I0770739

finer

Kerry Love

WRITER'S BLOCK

A blank piece of paper is my wall,
I think and think of nothing at all.
I sit and wait for the words to come.
I tap my pen, I start to hum.
I look around the room a bit,
I squirm and squiggle, then still I sit.
I have a thought, now I need a word,
So my ideas will be heard.
I wait and stare at the walls around.
For some, these are barracks,
For me, just something to lean on.
For a blank piece of paper is my wall.

Kerry Spengler
Age 13

ACKNOWLEDGMENTS

Writing is solitary work but editing, publishing, and distributing take a village. Special thanks to Juliet Ringhof, an amazing editor and a wonderful poet. I'm so grateful for your help.

To Alicia Welch, Kathleen Spengler, and Jill Houston, thank you for your feedback, editing, and constant support. I am not me without all of you.

Thanks to my family and friends- especially my friends that are family and my family that are friends.

To everyone who has ever supported me or my work by sharing, liking, buying, or even just an encouraging word, I appreciate you more than you know.

And to the stream, for having so much to say.

CONTENTS

CONTENTS

How are you we always ask
I am fine we say
And even if we're not fine
We say it anyway

But if we say we're not fine
Something shifts inside
That allows us to feel better
Than if we had just lied

Not fine is just fine
Because it's a place that is true
A place that has room
For the real me and you

And true is a place
Where we learn and we grow
Where we come face to face
With all we don't know

We're all just fine tuning
In this chaos called life
But just saying we're fine
Does not make it right

Maybe when we're honest
That none of this is fine
We can change the world
While we still have time

And remember our power
That we're the designer
When we speak the truth
We can build something finer

FINER

DUSK

As we allow ourselves to be transformed
So transforms our world

The creek is so low
Late summer low
You can smell the dank of the barely covered stones
But it is clear
And I can see the fish that have been hiding from me all spring
The dragonflies are big this time of year
And I have to lean forward on my perch
So that my toes
Painted late summer pink

LATE SUMMER LOW

Can bathe in the still cool water
Always cool water
Even in late summer
The shallow magic of the creek has me thinking
About what's next
What's next what's next what's next
As if it will not come
If I do not wait for it
Late summer is what's next
A hold-on season
Hold on to the time
When I can come down to the creek in sandals and still see a crawfish
In the water that's late summer low
When I rise at the same time to meet the sun
Yet she is running late
Spending more of her moments
Checking on the other side of the world
To see if they are ready
For her undivided attention
Does the crawfish wonder
What's next
Do the dragonflies or the fish
Or do they simply know
From the shift
Of the late summer sun

THE VIEW

If the next step on your path
Has not been laid before you
Look around you
And admire the view
Look *inside* you
And admire the view
Rest and listen and breathe
And just admire the view

SEAMS

I think the seams
Of this world
Are coming apart
Like so many pairs of pants
I've lost
Because of the way
My thighs kiss
When I walk
I'll keep wearing them though
And keep walking
And noticing
Where the seams
Of this world
Are coming apart

CHERISH

I am grieving
For another me
Letting go of who
I never got to be
My heart is aching
For a world I cannot see
Where love is loved
And free is freed
When time is kinder
And not a reminder
Of all we've lost
Especially our way
I'll look back
Upon this season
And cherish
Every single day

CURRENTS

In the time
After we met

          But before we were together
          When you were so far away
          And I wondered about it all

I would float
In the late afternoon
When the sun was starting

             To dip behind the house
                Making a line
             Down the middle of the pool

I would float
And let the artificial currents

                 Bounce me
                 Between

The sun and the shade
The light and the dark

             Until my skin had bumps
             And my fingertips ridges
       And there was only a sliver of sunlight left

But somehow the current
Would always return me there

                 To the light
             Until it was no more

UNCONTROLLABLE

He is old now
But his face is still young
Only the white eyelashes
On the eye that used to be black
Give him away
My grief gives me away
Always just below the surface
Uncontrollable
Like the bubbles of a rolling boil
I help carry him as he walks
His legs are his nemesis
The way the squirrels used to be
It is hard on both our bodies
My hands ache to my shoulders
We talk about his death
Sometimes I think it will be from murder
By my own aching hands
For the frustration I still get
At his stubbornness and the mess
He can't smell anymore
But that doesn't stop him from sniffing intently
And he still eats with gusto
When that goes
I think it will be time
Though I hope it's his choice
And not mine
His and death's
That they will slip away together
Some peaceful night

And I will come downstairs
To find my own devastation
And the guilt from my relief
I am crying even now
As I write this
Even though I know it is unlikely
These tears
Will spare me any future ones
I think untrue things like
I wish I knew how hard it was going to be
And pointless things like
I wonder how long we have left
We have spent nearly every day
Of fourteen years
Together
So much in love
That even strangers could see it
"He really loves you" they would say
And I really love him
But I never thought at 45
My only anchor to this world
Would be an aging and arthritic
Angel in a dog suit
Sometimes he's not there
He has gone elsewhere
While standing beside me
I pet him and whisper to him
That I am here, that he is safe
Come back to me, I say, we are together
And he still does for now
Yet in the same whisper that I ask him to stay
I tell him he can go
That I don't want him to suffer

He wants the same for me
So I try not to cry in his face
As I wonder about
Life without him
When the clouds roll in
As we putter around the park
I think it might not be so bad
If a lightning bolt
Took us both out
Together
It might be better
Than having to live without him
We know each other so well
That his thoughts are mine
But I hope he cannot hear my thoughts anymore
I hope he doesn't know
How often I think
Of closing my heart completely
So I never have to feel this way again
I think he'd be disappointed in me
Because if dogs are here
To teach us anything
It's that love is worth it
And that we are worth love
Our love is perfect
After all
A fingerprint like no other
Pressed into the ink of time
The lines a path
We will walk eternally
Side by side

S
O
M
E
T
I
M
E
S

Sometimes love, it finds you
And sometimes it is made
Sometimes love's the balm
And sometimes it's the blade
Sometimes love is feral
And sometimes it is tame
Sometimes love's a candle
And sometimes it's the flame
Sometimes love will leave you
And sometimes it will stay
But love is always worth it
There is no other way

It will be what you need
But not always what you want
Until what you need
And what you want
Become the same

THIS ONE

I know
(But cannot explain how)
It is written into the fabric
Of my being
In this world (not of it)
And in every world
That we will find each other
Again and again
Through all space
All time
In every world
Again and again
So there is no loss
No without
And yet
I can't help but want
More of you
In this one

S
INTER
C
T
E
D

You came over to show me
That I had to let you go
For that and for so many things
I'll always love you so
The hardest part for me now
As I step into the light
Is that even under smoke and fear
It's you who still smelled right
I can no longer see our future
But I'm not blinded by the past
I know love goes on forever
It's just time that doesn't last

LIKE DREAMS

There is an ache in my heart
That I named after him
There is one that I named
After you
I have hated and loved them
And filled them with light
I don't know what more I can do
They won't go away
No matter how much I try
So I'll keep on living
With these aches deep inside
And carry them around
Till the day that I die
Like dreams that never came true

If you decide who I am
Without learning who I am
I will destroy
The her you created

MANHOOD

If you are hating
            Women
You are doing manhood wrong
If you are hating
            Yourself
You are doing manhood wrong
If you are hating
            Life
            Others
            The world
    People who aren't like you
        And people who are
You are doing manhood wrong
If you are hating
You are hurting
And you are doing manhood
Wrong

If we called it Father Earth
Would you take better care of it
If I was a boy
Would you take better care of me

When you asked me
About Mary Magdalene
When you didn't know
Who she was
I realized
You didn't know who I was
That you mistakenly thought
I was your disciple
That martyrdom
Was your path
Silly boy
Silly fool
Go home Jesus
And release your need
To save anyone
But yourself

DISCIPLE

AGES

I loved my husband
As much as I
Could love anyone
Back in the dark ages
Of my heart
But I never needed him
Until I did
And learned the hard way
That it was not safe
To need a man
Who wouldn't let
Life change him

MAYBE THAT

The water is higher today
And it pushes up against
The banks of the creek
Full
Like the heart in my chest
Pushes up against
My rib cage
It is a joy to listen to
It is a joy to feel
How can it be
That only yesterday
The creek was so low
I loved it even then
Maybe that
Is what allowed it
To change

Becoming takes practice
Being is an art
You don't have to know
Where you're going
You only have to start

ALONE

I miss the voices in my head
I killed them all
I shot them dead
To try to live
Right here instead
And now I am
Alone

I have become a cult of one
It's only me
The rising sun
Shining bright
Nowhere to run
At last I am
Alone

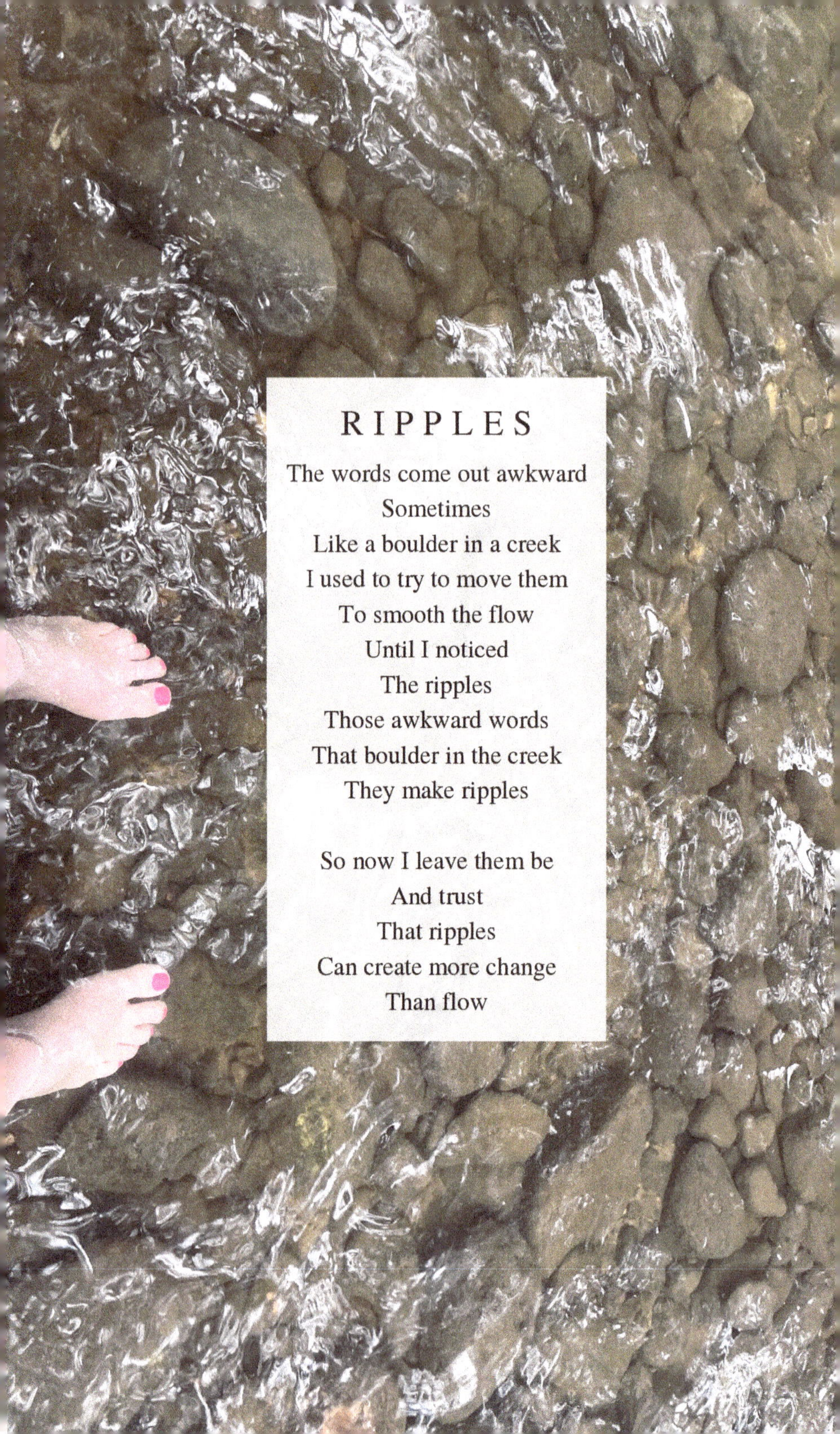

R I P P L E S

The words come out awkward
Sometimes
Like a boulder in a creek
I used to try to move them
To smooth the flow
Until I noticed
The ripples
Those awkward words
That boulder in the creek
They make ripples

So now I leave them be
And trust
That ripples
Can create more change
Than flow

I asked her what to do for you
When you lost your dad
She said I should write a poem
About loss
Like it was easy

Like it was easy
To find that thread of grief inside me
And touch the flame
The blue flame
So hot it's cold

Like it was easy
To tunnel through the layers of masks
The veneer of joy
Glued on with whispers
Of cheer
To find the thread
That electric current, always there
Humming softly
Burning cooly
Strong enough to cut through bone

Like it was easy
To find that thread
And dance around it
Even pluck it
Like a white hot guitar string
To see what note comes out

EASY

I do not know the grief
Of losing a dad
Only the grief of not really having one
And so I do not know your loss
Except for that burning thread inside me
The one that hums and whispers
Begging me to touch it
And remember
The pain
Of being without them
Like it was easy

I'm not perfect
But when I'm grateful
Everything else is

I heard this morning
>>That there was a gift for me
>>>>Down by the stream
Maybe I'll find a cool rock
>>>I thought
An old coin or a turkey feather
>>>>But I found nothing
And was disappointed to see
That the stream was not so full and joyous
As she had been the day before
>>>>There were no baby ducks
>>>There was no heron, great and blue

But I made my offering of rose petals
>>>>>Just the same
While I waited patiently for my gift
I watched how the sunlight
>>>Made a mirror of the water
Sparkling with the green
>>>>Of the trees above
The soft ripples
Whispered of what was underneath

>>>I put my feet in the cool
>>>>>But not frigid water
>>>And dragonflies danced around me
>>>I stared at the squirrel
>>>>>Who stared back at me
>>>Until I gave up waiting
>>>For my gift
>>>>>And walked home
>>>>Past the blooming roses
>>>>>With a full heart

EMPTY HANDED
>>>>>Empty handed

DROUGHT

The question asked
About my deepest
Darkest desires
And I found
That I had none
My darkness had
Shriveled up
From too much
Sun
And not enough
Rain
My heart closed
To drastic weather
Tired of the floods
Unaware
That I was instead
Creating
A drought
And I know
That is no way
For an artist
To live
No way to live
As a human
And so
I will begin
To dig a well
In this drought
Do a dance for rain
Until the water comes
And I am sated
With desire
Once again

You were not born
To walk a path
You were born
To forge one

Three docks I have walked
        To get to the river of love
One was washed away
        By a hurricane (of words)
            Never to be rebuilt
One became unsafe
    Disintegrated from lack of use
            And lack of care
One is still closed
            For repairs
    (It was at the time I walked it
        But I missed the signs)

So I no longer use docks
To get to the river of love   WADE
I found instead
    A gentle bank
            Inside me
                From which I can

                        w   a   d   e

                    in with care

    Or simply lie in the sun
            Beside the flowing water
    And pluck
    Any remaining splinters
                    From my feet

ALL ME

There is a ladybug
On a green branch
That looks like
It is about to bloom
And how is that possible
When tomorrow is November
And there was a freeze last night
I think this plant
Doesn't know
Whether it is blooming or dying
As the trees
Baptize the world
With the last of their leaves
The ducks in the creek
Have been preening
And less fearful
Blooming or dying
Preening and less fearful
A ladybug in fall
I can relate to it all
It is all me

Let your heart run wild
Let your mind be still
The mind was only ever meant
To serve the heart's will

NO MORE WORDS

There will be no more words
Written tonight
My love
You will have to read
I want you on my lips
Feel I love you from my eyes
Hear my nipples whisper their greeting
As they rise up to meet your touch
No there will be no more words
Written tonight
Only a moan in reply
To the questions of your tongue
And a sigh
That praises god

It is possible because you create it

COMMIT

As you commit
Everything
Wants your attention
Are you sure
Asks the world
Are you sure
Are you sure
Say yes
Just say yes
For you can always
Say yes
Again
To something new

PAST THE TIME OF COLOR

It is autumn
Past the time of color
I would have told you
If you asked
That I preferred the vibrant autumn
Before the leaves fell, or leapt
Or got blown off their branches
By a gust of chilly wind
The autumn of greeting cards
Red scarves and orange pumpkins
And lovers holding hands under golden trees
But only autumn past the time of color
Gives delicious crunching underfoot
While the few leaves that still hold on
Stubborn
Wave to me
Like my own
Sweet and slow heart
That also holds on
That also takes her time moving on
Because though things may be alike
They are never the same

Like autumn
And autumn past the time of color
When the nights encroach rudely
Into the day
And you find yourself passing
Through cool pockets of air
Like the cold spots in the ocean
A tide of nighttime chill creeping in
Long before the sun has set
Frigid as the day is warm

It is autumn
Past the time of color
The world grows stranger and stranger
With what it pretends to be real
I breathe and wait
For someone to flip the switch
And tell us the charade is over
That we can go back to loving
And caring for each other
Again
With the ease our hearts were born with
Most days it feels like the switch has already
Been flipped in me
The fuse of my fear and cynicism
Blown out by my gratitude
Never to be replaced
I don't mind operating
With the lights off
Especially if they were fluorescent
I prefer my light from fire anyway
The sun
The wick
Or within

I soften like sand
So I may change
With the tides
So my walls
Can be easily washed away
And not
Carved
Into a canyon

RIGHT NOW

It is a special time
This space between seasons
This pause before
The exhale
When the trees get their
Yellow freckles
But the rose bushes and
The tomato plants
Still have more to say
The magic of decay
Can be smelled faintly on the breeze
The chilly mornings
Warning us
To get outside in the still hot afternoon
And shine our faces toward the sun
Like great giant sunflowers

The stream is so cold on my feet
But I dip them in anyway
Because to miss a chance
That could always be my last
For the week, for the season
Forever
Seems foolish
Is foolish
And I've been a fool already
It is time for something
Different
I heard the browns and blacks
Of the wooly caterpillar
Can tell us how long winter will be
So I watch him intently
As he crosses my path
But come away knowing only
That everything is a miracle
On loan to us
For a short time
And I have been a fool to forget it
And I will be a fool again
But right now
I remember

DARK

Do not let people
Who don't believe in their own greatness
Make you doubt yours

THE DARKNESS

There is wisdom in the darkness
So let it call you near
This wisdom in the darkness
Is nothing you should fear
Your demons are not evil
They're just your hungry side
And when you get to know them
They can often be your guide
There is wisdom in the darkness
Holding something you should know
These pieces that don't see the light
Can show you how to grow
There is wisdom in the darkness
When it speaks give it a chance
It doesn't need to take the lead
It only wants to dance
So grab your darkness by the hand
And turn it toward the light
To see it, not to change it
There is no wrong or right

RIPEN

There is a gentle sadness
In my heart
When I notice how much earlier
The sun makes her descent
And the reluctance she begins to show
In her morning rise
When I notice the extra chill in the grass
As I walk barefoot to the garden
To pluck the tomatoes
Late in their abundance
And I think of my own life
Like the tomato plant
I am pregnant
Bowed humbly
By the many green fruit
What will come
What will come
And ripen in the waning sun

MOMENTS

There are moments
Where you are holding hands
With both the future
And the past
Moments where you cannot
Dwell
Moments where you must choose
To let one go
Or you will be
Torn
Apart

PURGATORY

Purgatory is what it feels like
In this place I used to call home
Where the sidewalks are lined
With shadows of neatly cut grass
Even at night
And I wonder if a shadow at night
Is as fake as the light that makes it
Or if it's just a different kind of real
Raised in this land of make believe
Where rockets sail overhead
And there are mice people want to hug
Where families bearing toothy grins speak with
Southern accents
Northern accents
No accents
What is the accent of purgatory
With its artificially frigid houses
Built atop a steaming swamp
That all look the same
The same mailboxes
The same driveways
Even the conversations are the same
With people who don't know anything
About themselves
Until someone else tells them
The only difference is the color
Of the identical crepe myrtles
In this place that used to smell
Of orange blossoms
And suntan lotion
But now reeks
Of confusion under a thin layer of rage

What does it mean
To be from purgatory
I guess it's as good
As anywhere else
Someone else's house
Someone else's life
Someone else's world
What does it mean
To be from purgatory
And what does it mean
That I belong there
No more

The sun is up
Steaming the world
Little black slugs with antennae
Like shell-less snails
Pepper the sidewalk
I sometimes try to pick them up
And put them in the grass
Before they are cooked by the sun
I walk past palm trees
And magnolias
With their giant waxy green leaves
And how can you pass a bird of paradise
Thinking you are in purgatory
You can't
Instead you remember
That everything is a miracle
Even little boxes made of ticky tacky
And purgatory is only as real
As the shadows
Of the grass at night

Anger is the birthright
Of every woman
When will you
Accept the gift

THE PUSH

I dreamed of you last night
That I pushed you from a tower

And you fell   (so surprised by my push)
        Without catching yourself

                I was surprised too
                I thought you might be dead
                And it horrified me
        Not your death   But the death of the me
                That *never* would have pushed you
        Shocked that my hands
                Which had caressed you so easily in one world
                        Could harm you so easily in another
        You were alive though
                With just the wind knocked loose from your lungs
And even though it was a dream
I don't think I did it
        To make you feel how I felt
                When you walked away from me
        But I also never thought
                        I had hands capable of
        The push

MARTYR

Do you ever take the best piece

Or do you leave it

For someone else

Do you allow yourself

To be worthy

Of what you want

Or do you choose less

In a silent (and pointless)

Demonstration

Of what?

Restraint?

Selflessness?

Generosity?

Do you ever take the best piece

Or do you forget yourself

And also, that the best piece

Is different

For everyone

Do you ever take the best piece

Or do you take someone else's

The winter cold will
Make you long
For the summer sun
You wasted

BOUND

The fish
Is not free
It is bound
To water
But it probably
Feels free
When it is
Swimming

I met a woman
Who had squandered her life
On being right
And thin and rich
Staying well-informed
And married
To both a world
And a man
That she did not seem to like
Chaining herself to the righteous table of
What Other People Think

SQUANDERED

One by one
Everyone else at the table
Got up to leave
Until she was the only person left
Waiting for her prize
Alone
She didn't seem to notice that she wasn't happy
Maybe to her
Right and happy
Were the same
I met a woman
Who had squandered her life
On being right
And I was glad to be reminded
Not to become her

You're trying to save others
While you're drowning
Save yourself
Because there are no
Others

THE FEED

There are people on my feed-
Feed feed feed
Social media is a feed lot
And we are prematurely fattened cattle
Being readied to feed something
Larger and more grotesque
In this feed lot filled
With truth and lies-
But there are people on my feed
These good people
Yelling at me
To care about dead babies
And I do
I have been crying about dead babies
Since I was born
Since I was a dead baby
My childhood killed
By the distorted pain of grown men
I felt like I was the only one alive
In my classes at school
Sobbing alone
While we watched Roots
And Dances with Wolves
Do you not know our history
Littered with dead babies
Did you not know
Until it was in your feed
Feeding you
Outrage

There is nothing casual
About casualties of war
Especially babies
(And we are all babies)
In these atrocities labeled as tragedies
One after another
I sign petitions and I donate
And I wonder how much more of my life
To give to dead babies
On days when I think of being shot
In my classroom
I know I would give it all
And if you could tell me
It would save anyone
Or anything
To feed the feed
With more outrage
I would gladly do it
Maybe because none of my babies
Were ever even given a chance to live
Maybe that's why all children
Have always felt like mine
So I would gladly
Feed the feed
If it would help
And be fed
With the outrage
If it would help
I'd let it pour over me
Drowning me
In the insanity of bloodshed
How can we be surprised
When it has always been like this

And how does my drowning
Serve anyone
How would my outrage
Add any nourishment
To the feed
I know there are dead babies
They are everywhere in this world
I have seen them
I have carried them
I have killed them
I have been them
How many more lives
Must I give
How many more moments
Of this one
Even on my walks
The ones I take to remember why I'm here
To witness all of the beauty
That reminds me it's worth it
I cannot stop and admire
The exquisite columbine
Without thinking of dead babies
If I thought any of it would help
If one drop from the feed
Would save even a baby goldfish
I would do it
But the feed is not a drop
It's a fire hydrant
And my drowning
Would only leave my mother
With another
Dead baby

It is easy to blame my sadness
On you being gone
The wound keeps bleeding
When you pick it all the time

DOWNSTREAM

Sometimes
Even when it's beautiful
I feel like
I am just holding on

Trying to keep my head
Above water
Trying to keep from

Drowning

Forgetting
I know how to swim
And if I just let go
That I could even
Float
Downstream
To all the magic
That awaits me

THE GRIEF

It is a frigid stream
(The grief)
That I sit on the banks of
Day after day
I cannot survive without drinking from it
Without slipping one foot into
The icy water
Brisk and painful
And refreshing
I am alive
As it rushes by in front of me
And through the center of me
I see it and I feel it and I am it
So there is no hiding
Only tuning out
To make room for laundry
And emails
Words and tea
How long can a heart break for
How long can I go
Without taking a drink

OH MY

A thunderstorm is coming
Oh my how I loved him
It's moving in fast
Oh my how I loved him
I'm thinking bout the past
Oh my how I loved him
My heart is breaking open
Lightning splitting me in two
Rain pouring down my face now
No hope is shining through
Oh my how I loved him
Oh my how I loved him
It's over in a moment
The clouds parting up above
This storm has left a place for
A deeper kind of love

The worst mistakes I've ever made
Have been
The same ones

THAT IS

I stood on the rain soaked grass
Under an awning of lilac branches
And peered up at the sun
Please help me release the lover
That isn't meant for me
And embrace the one that is
Please help me release the life
That isn't meant for me
And embrace the one that is
Please help me release the moment
That isn't now
And embrace the one
That is

WEALTH

The stream was loud today
So full of gab
About last night's rain
And though it was murky
And I could no longer see
The rocks below
I was happy to hear
Its bubbling joy
At the wealth of movement

HAIKU OF A LONELY POET

I want you to come
over here and give me some
thing to write about

THE UNFOLDING

I'm scared
Not of you
But of the me in us
I'm scared
That I jinxed the whole thing
By telling people that you even exist
And I'm scared of how easily a crumb of doubt
Shakes my faith
How quickly my mind gets
To the conclusion that
Cutting and running
Are the best thing
The smart thing
The right thing
I'm scared that I will listen
Because I have always wanted to be
Smart and right
And because that voice in my mind
Is often so much louder
Than the one in my heart
Whispering
Be patient, be patient, be patient
The simple wisdom
That allows for the grace
Of the unfolding
But if I don't run
I'm scared of how
I will morph and change
To meet your needs

And of how little I will accept
In return
Pretending to be fine
While resentment grows
Like poison ivy in my gut
Because I'm scared you don't really know me
Don't really see me
That you just need someone to hold your hand
Right now
And you think I feel safe
But I'm scared that I am the furthest thing from it
(Safe)
That the banshee inside of me
Wants to break free
And tell you all the things
You could be doing better
When she doesn't know
But I've heard the banshee before
And she does know some things
Like where your softest spots are
And I'm scared that if she feels
Hurt or neglected one more time
She will come out and burn this whole thing down
And I will be devastated
Wondering what could have been
And I'm scared that if I hold her back
To protect you
To save you
She will devour me instead

You wanted my body
And I wanted you
It's not the same to love
As it is to do

UNMET

I want to tell you
That my body misses your body
But I'm afraid
It will make you curl into yourself
And away from me
The way it feels like you did
The last time I spoke of my needs
Still unmet
I can't remember the last time
You said I love you
And not just I love you too
I don't know if I should
Wonder what that means
Or just breathe
I'm afraid to ask
If the way we love each other
So freely outside the frame
Means we are building a solid foundation
Or just letting each other drift
Further apart
Until we end up in different currents
I don't know
But I do know
That my body misses your body
That I love you
And I love you too
That I am
Still breathing

I
need
to be

Fed and
stoked

And tended
Like a fire

And for the
same reason

So that I may
provide

Warmth
and
light

L
I
K
E

A

F
I
R
E

Leave me alone
Long enough

And I will remember

That I am

Better company

Than you

Ever were

BETTER

NOT ALL MEN

It has been a long journey
Coming home from hating men
Of course, they have not been all bad
Men
Not all men
Though it was hard for me to see
The ones by my side
When my head was being forced
To look at the ones in front of me
Forced attention is still attention
(and some people's favorite kind)
So it has been a long journey
But a hopeful one
A worthwhile one
To remove the hands from my head
The gag from my mouth
The vice from my heart
To turn my neck and see
The truth
Of the amazing men who have held me up
(Not often
 But when I've let them)
Escorting me, exquisitely
Home to myself

Of shooting stars
I saw just two
One for me
And one for you

ADVENT

Tis the season to reflect
On what has gone and what comes next
To thank the gods or just your soul
For privileges of growing old
For wisdom found through what we've lost
For things we made and what they cost
For battles fought and lives now broken
For things we've said and left unspoken
All of it has made us grow
The rain, the sun, the wind, the snow
Every moment time well-spent
To birth anew on this advent

I listen to the ones that know more than me
They are the ones that claim to know less
I humble myself before the trees
I bow down to the stream
I hold tight to the feather
And I listen
I listen

I LISTEN

UNBIDDEN

How many times
Have I sat by this creek
How many poems written
Here
And only today
Did I have the thought
Unbidden but timely
That the creek has always been
The one writing the poems
I am just
Holding the pen

The moon is spicy tonight
She makes me dizzy just to
Look at her
With my feet in the cool earth
I can smell the world around me
So clearly
The pine and the grass
And the laundry detergent
Of the men that I walk past
Saunter really
Hips swaying
Belly round
Full of toast and tea
And every dream
About to burst forth
Come through me
Come to me
Come in me
(I told you she is spicy)
She whispers of my power
This moon, this luna picante
And she washes away my fear
Leaving me bare
But not naked
Full
But still wanting
Alive and unafraid

SPICY

I am safe in the forest
Because
I am
The forest
Both of us wild
And reaching for
The light

THE FOREST

DAWN

Magic is everywhere
It doesn't care if you believe in it
But you will never recognize it
Until you do

I'M ALIVE

Walking in the spring is orgasmic
Like most things are
If you do them right
You cannot be in a hurry
Or distracted
No, walking in the spring
Requires focus
A gentleness of foreplay
Insistent attention
Otherwise you will miss
The robin by the rushing stream
Or the worm peeking out from under the grass
The caterpillar that saunters by
And the ducks that give side-eye
As they swim off to somewhere more private
Even the little mouse
And the cricket
Call out to be seen
As if everything in the woods
Shares the same chorus
Notice me
I am alive

The one who walks first
must make friends with the spiders

MIRROR

Why do you do that
Don't you see
We're so different
You and me

Your clothes aren't like mine
Your skin's not my color
There's no way that we
Could be like one another

But when you lift your arm
My arm lifts up too
Are we really so different
Not sure that is true

Who hasn't been broken
By grief and by loss
No one learns the lessons
Without paying the cost

We may live our lives different
But we love just the same
Our world is in shambles
And I think we're to blame

I lift my arm up
You lift your arm too
When we come together
The world starts anew

I can hear our story
            I can hear it
                The way a bee can hear
                    The petals of a flower
                        Start to unfurl
Not through sound
            But vibration

WIGGLING

If you watch clearly
In the spring
You can see the trees
Wiggling
With new growth
If you watch closely
In the spring time
You can see me
Do the same

The creek feels good today
Hearty but not overwhelmed
Lively but not boisterous
I feel the same
Leaving pieces of me behind
The stones from a broken bracelet
Made by friend
Back in a broken life
Stones that came from the earth
Returned
Polished with grit and magic
An offering
And a letting go
Old for new
Thanks for please
I watch the ripple
The beads make
As I drop them in
One by one
Ripples no one will see
Imprints of a moment
Yet somehow like
The wings of the butterfly
Half way around the world
Maybe they are
Changing everything

RETURN

It is almost time
To leave this place
This creek which has nourished me
As surely as the ducks and the fish
The trees and the snakes
I don't know if I will be here again
I have left enough lives behind
To know
That even if I were to return
There is no coming back

When we listen to one another
Really listen
What we will hear
Is the sacred story of
This is how I got through

MELTING

It was sunny today
The kind of sunny
That melts off enough snow
To leave patches of green grass
Exactly the kind of day you would have loved
So many layers of scents melting together
Exactly the kind of day
That snuck up on me
When I turned the corner into the park
To find the first kind of that day
Without you
I was surprised how fast a golf ball grew in my throat
(Like the ones you used to chase)
My whole body hurt for missing you
And I cried hard
Standing there alone in the park
Until my eyes were clear enough to see
That those days
Are not gone
That I am in the park with you
Still
Always
That the joy of those moments
Can only be taken from me
By me
And I knew grief a little deeper then
The scent of it melting into me
Like the snow into the grass

We became more intimate in that moment
Grief and I
He whispered to me
That he would never really be gone
Nor would you
That he would always be there to sneak into some moment
Surprising me with another layer of tears
Melting onto my cheeks
And I felt more human than I ever had
Like I had unlocked a deeper layer of being
Of knowing
I cried a little more for how resilient we are
Every human on this planet
Wells of melted grief
How are we still breathing?
The people who have lost parents
And siblings
Still breathing
The people who have lost lovers
And friends
Still breathing
And my god
How are people still breathing
After losing a child
It must feel like their whole bodies
Are covered in shards of glass
Cutting them with every move
Every memory
The layers of all our grief
Melting into the world
While we are still breathing
And yes, he was just a dog
Just a partner, just a home
And I
I am just a human

It's strange
How the future
Can be so bright
That it scares you
Back
Into the past

And how now
I can notice
Pause
Stretch
Expand
To hold it all

Hope in one hand

Grief in the other

Tethering me
To this world

So I don't

Float

AWAY

You matter
You matter
You matter
And if you should forget
Remind another

STAY

When I couldn't bear this world
And still remain right here
I had to rise above it all
The hate, the doubt, the fear

And there I found it waiting
For you and just for me
The place beyond the right and wrong
That heaven claimed to be

There's still rain and sun and rainbows
Even though we've lost so much
We still can see each other
We still can feel and touch

Though nothing lasts forever
We get each and every day
The chance to make life better
If we only choose to stay

There's somewhere better waiting
It comes from deep inside
Your heart is what creates it
When you dare to open wide

I fell for you
The way the rain
Falls from a cloud
Because it is so full
And the earth below so

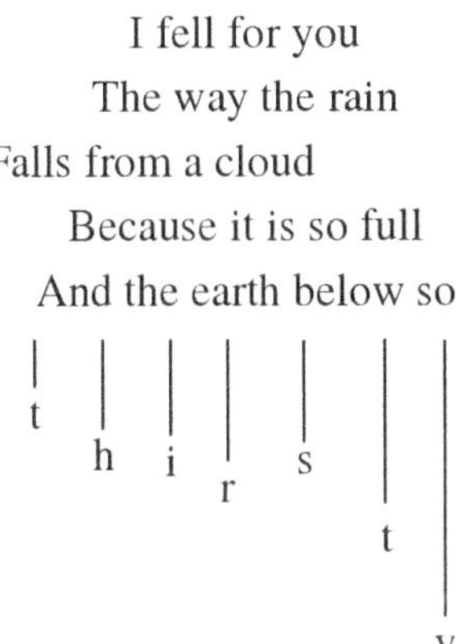

It is spring
And I am alone
On the deck   WATER ME
In the rain and sun
The first sunshower
I have ever seen in Colorado
So I am sitting in the moment
Another moment alone
                Another season without a lover's tongue
                                Slipping between my lips
                        A lover's hand between my thighs
And how can I be lonely in a moment
As perfect as this
A sunshower
In Colorado
Raining down on my lips
Still sweet from the mango
Or the chocolate
Standing between hemispheres
Of blue sky
                        And dark clouds
Bathing in the inherent balance
                        Of the chaos that is spring

Composing poems about
Letting go of trying to let go
Searching for a peace
                        That only comes from the moment
And therefore can never be found
                                By searching

It is sublime
      This springtime loneliness
With the sun so bright
      And the rain so cold
And the happy grass dancing
In this desert where it would perish
Without help from sprinklers

And I find my loneliness again
As the child of my heart whispers

Water me
I cannot always water myself

It is spring
And I am alone

I had the saddest thought today
While sitting on the porch
Thinking of the clone army you told me about
When I asked you about Star Wars
Not because I really wanted to know about Star Wars
But because I wanted to spend time
Listening to the version of you
That loves it
The same reason I like to listen
To you talk about me
But before I could make a mental note to ask you
Post-its in the hurricane of my mind
I answered my own question
Like I try to do with everything
So I never have to need
Anybody
So I can always
Keep my heart
Just a little bit closed
Not because that has ever
Kept anyone safe
Especially not me
But because it's a habit
I don't know how to break
The same way I don't know how the good guys
Defeat the clone army in Star Wars
But I know how we do it here
In this wicked world
We teach them how to love
Of course

THE SADDEST THOUGHT

Of course
We will have to learn first ourselves
Which brings me back
To the saddest thought I had today
When I was wondering about
Good versus evil
In movies I may never watch
Set in a world I may never see
I thought
What if the waitress
At the airport restaurant
That I wasn't going to go to
Two hours before I was never going to be there
What if she hadn't sat me
Across
From you

I wonder

how I can miss you

so badly

Nobody sane

misses

A hurricane

FOOL ME ONCE

I went courting with the mist one day

When the sun arose he went away

Like the frost you find on an autumn leaf

Like the air exhaled from lungs of grief

Like the notes of a song you can barely hear

The tilt of my head made him disappear

The first walk with the mist was nice

Shame on me for going twice

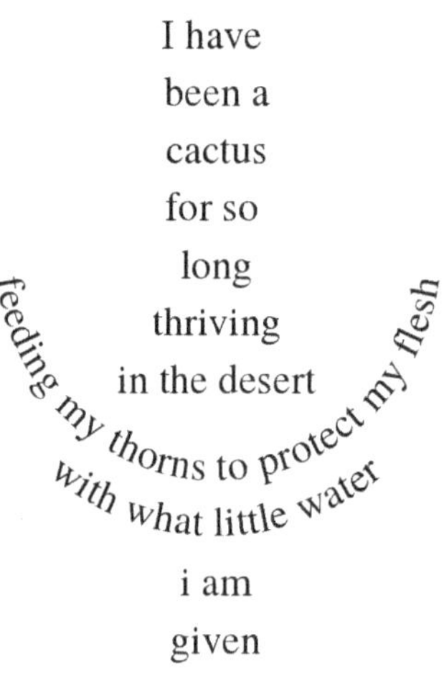

I have
been a
cactus
for so
long
thriving
in the desert

i am
given

CACTUS

How many times do you have to let go?
One more than you have held on

MORE THAN ONE

I have been lost for a year
Without him
Yet he always finds me
More times than I can count
In some black and white animal
Or the smell of cornflakes
Or St. Roco's Hermitage
When I turn the corner
Of a narrow street
In a small town in Spain
He finds me always
Though I still feel so lost
That probably means something
But my eyes are too blurry with tears
To see what
A small pond compared to the oceans
I have cried
Since he's been gone
And before
The end so hard and long
But somehow not long enough

People may think it's silly
That my grief could still be so big
For an old dog that's been gone so long
But maybe it's more silly to imagine
You know what it's like
To be anyone else
Plus I've finally gotten better
At not caring
Whether I make sense to other people
Some days
I don't even make sense to myself
It's a fool's errand anyway
Making sense
And I may still act like a child
But I have never been a fool
Except for that dog
And a few other dogs
Wandering around as men
I know now
That he was the great
Love of my life
For I have never loved anything like him
Then, or since
But maybe there can be
More than one
Maybe
There will be more

Maybe all you really need
Is someone next to you
Reminding you
That it's safe to bloom

BIRDS

I need you
Like birds need trees
But like birds need feathers
Is how I need me
I need you
Like birds need spring
I need me
Like birds need wings
I need you
Like birds need the sky
But I need me
Like birds need to fly

Nobody can give you faith
Which means nobody can take it away

YOURSELF

When was the last time
You sat with yourself
Listened to your own breath
Treated your time
For what it is
Sacred

When was the last time
You nourished yourself
Fed the flames of your own heart
Treated your desire
For what it is
Holy

When was the last time
You anointed yourself
Cherished your own flesh
Treated your body
For what it is
Miraculous

It's taken me years
But I've come to see
I have never been wronged
It has always been me   ALWAYS
No matter what's happened
Or who took the fall
It's always been me
So I just love it all

DANCE

In this dance of life
At this masquerade
Though the costumes change
While the music plays
No matter how we dance
Under stars above
We are always held
In the arms of love

A bigger wave
May move more sand
But a thousand tiny waves
Can also change a coastline

COSTCO

There is nothing to celebrate
Because we have
Everything
To celebrate
These days
Giant bags of dark chocolate covered mangoes
A revelation
A hymn
Pure magic
That I only sometimes remember
To celebrate
All of the rain and the sun
That needed to drench the earth
For my tongue to be
Drenched in this pleasure
In a bag so big from Costco
That I only notice them
When they are gone

I can't draw you a map
But I can show you
How to build a compass

EXPENSIVE

It is too easy to spend
Your nows
On the future
Or scatter them behind you
In the past
If your nows
Were more expensive
You could make
The moment last

Peace is knowing your truth
Wisdom is understanding that it's yours alone
Growth is allowing it to change
When it no longer brings you peace

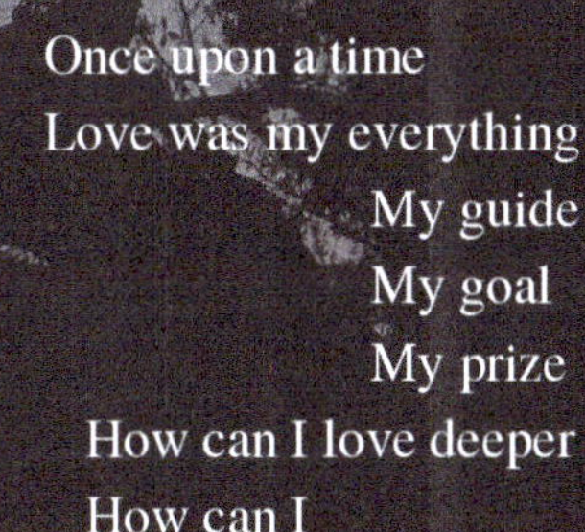

Once upon a time
Love was my everything
My guide
My goal
My prize
How can I love deeper
How can I
Seek love
Find love
Make love

How can I give
More of myself
All of myself
To love love love

I loved so much
I wore myself thin
Like the fabric of a favorite shirt
Or the corner of an old baby blanket
Frayed and about to come undone

So now
While the world teases out
Real love
From control
I walk away
Sit in a rocker on my porch
And choose peace
That is where
Love will find me

FIND ME

All of it is right

None of it is wrong

Whatever season you're in

That's where you belong

But seasons change

As most things do

And so will change

Both me and you

SEASONS

PRACTICING

I sat very still when I saw
The momma duck and her babies
       Only moving my eyes to close them
      And wish her peace
        To permeate the space we shared
        With safety
She accepted my gift
       And in return allowed me to watch
     As she and her babies swam closely by me
I nearly cried for my joy
Of her trust in me
       That she could sense I was safe
Because I am practicing all the time
      Being safe
     I am practicing
     For you

There is no there
Only *here*
There is no then
Only *now*
There is no them
Only *us*
How can you make it better
How will you
Make it better

ONLY

A GAME

I watched a reality show today
Two small fierce birds
Squawked
And chased a young hawk
From their nest
A rabbit remained still
Hiding from it all
Under a bush
While the cottonwoods
Tinkled with laughter
A funny soundtrack
That reminded
Every one of us
It's only
A game

THE TRYING

She thought she could heal him
And so let him break her
   In the trying
He thought he could save her
And so let her drown him
   In the trying

She thought she could love him
And so learned to save herself
   In the trying
He thought he could love her
And so learned to heal himself
   In the trying

They thought they could change
And so changed the world
   In the trying

DAY

Great changes happen when
Wild Dreamers
Let their love loose in the world

Who knew the apocalyptic sun would be so beautiful
That giant red orange ball appeared low in the sky
So I did not linger when I saw her
The sun
Making her morning ascent
I wanted to witness her brilliance
And spare my lungs
So I turned my back to the creek
Put on my broken shoes
And walked through the smokey air
Forest fires from a thousand miles away
Whispering their farewell over a city
That those trees have never seen
Mingled of course
With the smoke from engines
All that exhaust
Exhausting
As I made my way home
Past the flowers
Some sun burnt

APOCALYPSES

Some still blooming
Even in an apocalypse
They will be gone soon
As will we
Only to be reborn
There is nothing to fear
Everything ends
Even apocalypses

As I fall in love
With imperfection
Everything becomes
Perfect

No one calls
The rose wise
Beautiful, yes
Fragrant and lovely, yes
But if she were not
Also wise
Would she grow
Thorns

LEAF BLOWERS

Today I tried to love leaf blowers
Intrusive and pointless
As they are
Because the moment full of beautiful blue sky
And warm breezy sunshine
Also contained
Leaf blowers
Aggressively
Unbearably
Loud
So I decided to take a stand
And fight for my peace
By loving the whole moment
Even the leaf blowers
While quietly building
A world without
Them

Do not forget!
I want to shout to my students
As they leave my class
(Like I am some accidental Peter Pan
Staying behind in Neverland)
Please don't forget!
To be who you are
To keep the piece of yourself
You found here
The loud world will try hard
To make you forget
With jobs and babies
And dishes and time
But don't forget
My children
All of you beautiful children
To be all of you
And more
And when you forget
(Not if, when, because you will
We all do)
Come back to
The quiet world
Come back to stillness
Come back to the place
In your heart
Where I will always live
Come back
And I will remind you

COME BACK

THE NEWS

I watched the news today
The crows were convening
To complain about the previous gray days
It's as good a reason as any
To come together and celebrate this sunny one
Because sweet tastes even better
With a little bit of salt
The sandhill cranes reported
In their dinosaur voices
About how they saw me dance down a runway
And rescue a plastic bag
Before it could be distributed
To another place where it did not belong

They never said where it would end up
And I tried not to think about that
Or my complicity in any of it
I do what I can
It's all I can do
And still want to smile at strangers
And dance down abandoned fairways
Airstrips that used to be the landing ground for golf balls
The tri-colored heron was on the scene
And brave enough to go live in the middle of the action
As curious about me as I was about him
While the ducks floating in the swimming pool
Gave the weather report
Unseasonably warm and breezy for December
They said with their contentment
And beckoned me to join them
But I know my Colorado blood
Is no match for my Florida bones
So I turn my attention to the great old oak trees
Wearing their Spanish moss
Like they too are decorated for the holidays
Reminding us all
That every day
Is worth celebrating

I was in love
With the promise of you
I didn't realize
Until I got your email
Telling me that you loved my work
(I knew you would)
But that you were married
I thanked you for being a class act
And told you that just putting myself out there
Felt like a win
What I didn't tell you
Was that I surprised myself with tears
When I got your message
Realizing
That I like being in love
With the promise of someone
The blank pages
Ready to be filled
I think I have always been in love
With blank pages
So maybe the tears
Were not from the loss
Of the promise of you
But the unashamed
And joyful
Welcome home
To another piece of
The promise of me

B L A N K
P A G E S

COMPELLED

Whatever is between us
Has become so strong
That at certain moments
I am compelled
To surrender to it
To stop what I am doing
And melt into myself
Where I find you waiting
So strange is it
To know how you feel
But not who you are
So strange is it
That a moment out of time
Can hold your past
And your future
Without you knowing either
So strange is it
That something can feel both impossible
And inevitable
Elusive and concrete
Missing and found
There is nothing between us
There is nothing between us

Did I kiss you
                    Or did you kiss me

          My eyes were closed
            I didn't see

Did you kiss me
                    Or did I kiss you

            We're mirrors now
            I guess both are true

THIS LOVE

Is This Love
Was playing
When he first kissed me
I held onto that
So close
For so long
Like somehow that would
Make it love
Like I could weave a life
From a moment

I don't know what was playing
When you first kissed me
Maybe because
With you
I never needed to ask
Is this love

When he asked me if I was in love
I didn't know what to say
Does it mean that I'm in love with you
If I think of you all day

TWO KINDS

There are two kinds of love
I love you
And *I love you too*
One not better than the other
They both belong
In each of you

I can make
An ocean of love
From a single drop
Transform an ember
Of hope
Into a shooting star
Create a lifetime of dreams
From a moment
In your eyes
I am a woman
That way

THAT
WAY

DIVINE

I see so many
Things in you
Things you can't
But still are true
Things you're hiding
From yourself
For some that's love
For some it's hell

And here we are
In a prison
Of our words
While our hearts
Laugh
Outside

RAMEN FOR ONE

I am eating ramen for one
At a corner table in the sun
Where are you
You should be here
Across from me
So we can laugh
About the version of Tom's Diner playing
In a language we don't know
Or maybe you would know
You often surprise me with the things you know
I guess I thought that I would always be one of them
But you don't even know I started taking singing lessons
Where I just accidentally brought you up
Let the memory of you slip in
How could it not
I am always one unguarded heartbeat away
From your memory slipping in
So now it sits here across from me
While I'm eating ramen for one
At a corner table
In the setting sun

Nothing is ever always

MY OLD LIFE

My old life
Doesn't recognize me anymore
It cannot find me
By my voice
Can no longer hear my complaints
It cannot find me
By my fear
Can no longer feel my anxiety
When it looks for me now
In the field where I would toil
It will only find
A patch of wildflowers
Where my shadow used to lay

99

I dropped my moral
Compass
And it smashed onto the ground
Broke into a hundred

p i e c e s

But only
99 were found

A MUSE

Maybe he told her
And maybe he didn't
Maybe he keeps the secret of me
Hidden in his wallet
For him and only him
To take out
Unfold
And look over
Now and then
I don't mind much either way
He was never mine
Nor did I want him to be
But maybe she'll see
What I wrote
And think I love him
Because I see him
In a way
She never has

ANYTHING

The hummingbird's feet
Are drawn with the finest tip
Lines so slender, impossibly slender
They can barely be seen
How do they perch on something so tiny
Then I think of ant legs
And gossamer bumblebee wings
And wonder how we can possibly
Think we know
Anything

THE TRUTH

Sometimes when people lie to you
It's because they are vile
And duplicitous and
Human
And sometimes
It's because
You were not
A safe space
For the truth

BABY DUCKS

If I wrote about
Baby ducks when I see them
I would not see them

Let your heart
Always be
A little greedier
Than your mind
Let it love as much
As it can
As many
As it can
Don't let the mind
Convince you
It's unsafe
Gorge yourself on love
Until you are so full
You overflow

GREEDY

Send avalanches of love
Cascading down mountains
Let great mudslides of love
Wash away any walls
Left around your heart
Allow fiery sprays of love lava
To rain down on you
Then cool the burns with
Thunderstorms of love
And after it all
Love will apologize
With an abundant harvest
Of fruits and flowers
And joy
For you to sit down
Rest
And gorge yourself again

Does a raindrop
  Wonder how to fall
Or a stream
  Which way to flow
Does a wave
  Ask how to crest and break
Or the snow
  Which way to blow
Does a waterfall
  Ask how it should move
Or the tides
  When they should rise
Does steam
  Ask how to take to air
Or tears
  To fill your eyes
Water always knows
Where it should go
                And you are
                Mostly water

MOSTLY
WATER

Firm up where you have been lax
Soften where you have been rigid
Then let go of the idea
That you have to do
Either

Become a devotee
Of one
Not the guru
Not the shaman
And certainly not
The politician or the priest
Listen to others
Not for
The way
But like you are
Panning for gold
Sifting out only
What is precious
To you
There will be many
And they may speak loudly
Their path may shine brightly
As they beckon you to follow
It may be tempting
To hand your power
To someone so certain
It may feel safer
To be told who you are
But this
This is when you must
Sit
Be still
Be quiet
Be you
And become
A devotee
Of one

DEVOTEE

WILD

I am calm but feral
I am loving and wild
I'm a full grown woman
Who didn't get to be a child
So if you find me in the woods
Talking to something you can't see
It doesn't mean I'm crazy
It only means I'm free

BEND

There is a
b
e
n
d
in
the
creek
That didn't used to be there
The birds caw wildly
To get my attention
To help me notice
That even though
I have walked this way
Many times before
Nothing
Is the same

My lover knows my secret
That I'm changing every hour
My lover knows the balance
Between savor and devour

WHEN

Will you love me
When I'm an old lady
Who drinks tea
In her rocking chair
And speaks to the birds
As if they were her friends
When I am moving more slowly
Because time grows short
And I must notice everything
When I will only ever wear
Comfortable shoes
And let words fall from my mouth
That maybe I should have kept in

Will you love me
When I wander off without my phone
Eat dinner at five
And get into bed at nine
When I forget what day it is
How to work my computer
What I was going to say
Will you love me
When I run from you
Even though I really want
Connection

Will you love me
When I get it right
And
When I get it all wrong
When I'm better than you
And when I'm worse
Will you love me
With food stuck to my face
And ink-stained hands
And leaves in my hair

Will you love me
Now

I have been watching my life
The same way I watch football
These days
Half paying attention
Not getting too invested
In one outcome or the other
Certain that will give my team
A better chance at victory
My nonchalance the magic ingredient
The secret in the sauce
I have been watching football
These days
The same way I watch my life
Hoping for a win
But knowing
It will be okay either way
Either way
It will be okay

EITHER WAY

CONTENT

I sit by the stream
And let it tell me
Who I am these days
I thought about
Picking old scabs
Poking scars
But I don't need to do that
To feel alive anymore
If there are apologies
Well, I will make them
When it's time
If it's time
I've done my best to lay those stories
To rest
I'm only interested
In the one that is unfolding right now
Before my eyes
Two fat squirrels
Climbing high into the branches
Pulling off pieces
Chewing them
And letting them fall

I ask the stream what they are doing
If they are nature's pruners
As well as her planters
But the stream only bubbles in reply
And I realize I don't much care
To know why
Maybe it is enough
To just watch them
And listen to the stream
Who has been whispering the secret
All along
"You are learning to be content"
Even the one who has me grinning
Only crosses my mind for a moment
I am learning to be content
Even when the black and white dog
A visiting memory
Sure to break my heart
Stops to say hello
I can only smile
There is no heartbreak here
I'd be lying if I said
I didn't miss it
And I'd be lying if I said I did
It's a funny place to be
Content
As I am learning

Our souls
Yours and mine
Know nothing
Of time

TWO
LEAVES

And then I see them
Two leaves
Coming toward each other
Intertwining
Moving together
As they float downstream
As one
And I know what is next for me
Even if I don't know
Who or how
I am thankful

EPITAPH

I can't stop writing
But if I could
My final words
Will not be *should*
I won't hope for more
I won't wish for less
I accept it all
This holy mess
There'll be no talk
Of stars above
My final word
Will just be
LOVE

you are here

EPILOGUE

Some sleepy Sunday
When we've talked about everything else
You will ask me
Who I wrote
All those poems for
And I will answer truthfully
When I say
You
They were always
Just for you

About the Author

Kerry Love is a writer and an artist. She was the little girl who used to write stories for fun and read books under her covers with a flashlight, long after bedtime.

Also by Kerry Love:
By Chance (with Jill Cammack)
Not Fine
Fine Tuning

kerrygretchenlove.com
@kerrygretchenlove